ECHO CHAMBER

Also by Renee Norman

House of Mirrors 2001
True Confessions 2005

Backhand Through the Mother 2007

Martha in the Mirror 2010

Hearing Echoes 2016, co-authored with Carl Leggo

ECHO CHAMBER

RENEE NORMAN
& CARL LEGGO

Editor: Susan Musgrave
Cover image and design: Julie Van Huizen
Book design: Courtney Hellam
Printed and bound in Canada at Rapido Books, Montreal, QC

The publisher gratefully acknowledges the support of the Canada Council, Ontario Arts Council and the Canadian Government.

Canada Council for the Arts Conseil des arts du Canada
ONTARIO ARTS COUNCIL CONSEIL DES ARTS DE L'ONTARIO
an Ontario government agency un organisme du gouvernement de l'Ontario
Canada

Library and Archives Canada Cataloguing in Publication

Title: Echo chamber / Renee Norman and Carl Leggo.
Names: Norman, Renee, 1950- author. | Leggo, Carleton Derek, 1953-2019, author.
Identifiers: Canadiana (print) 2025027812X | Canadiana (ebook) 20250278154
ISBN 9781834210131 (softcover) | ISBN 9781834210209 (EPUB)
Subjects: LCGFT: Poetry.
Classification: LCC PS8627.O763 E34 2025 | DDC C811/.6—dc23

INANNA PUBLICATIONS & EDUCATION INC.
www.inanna.ca
TORONTO, ONTARIO, CANADA

Inanna Publications and Education Inc.
210 Founders College
York University
4700 Keele Street
Toronto, ON M3J 1P3
Canada

For my loving & remarkable daughters Sara, Rebecca, & Erin
(again, always)
who fill my life with joy & delight.

And for my precious grandchildren Frances, June, Ellee, Anna & Alistair,
who remind me daily of the bonds of love,
the wonder & restorative powers of hugs & smiles,
& the importance of snacks and surprises.

Contents

Part IV: STILL WRITING

Note: Throughout the book Renee Norman's poetry appears in sans serif font, and Carl Leggo's poetry in serif font.

SONG AND POETRY IN THE ECHOES

Before Valerie died, she reminded me
how I once advised her, learn to sit
for an hour on a bench and do nothing,
and know love is the answer to all
the questions. Good advice, even
if I don't practice it
Carl Leggo

Carlsong

(for Carl, who first called me poet and writer)

25 years
2 hips and a knee ago
I first met Carl
long hair pulled back
hanging down
a cream fisherman knit sweater
the cadence of an Eastern sea
fish boats
in his lilting rhythms

and now
my metal parts set off alarms
which joint
will next join the clamour?

I look through my files
Swedish pre-death clean-up
my daughters shouldn't have to,
so many multiple copies
seems I have a copying habit

out go the nasty comments:
student course evaluations
old graduate study notices
definitely the page from Carl:
"your thesis draft is too long"
stated 5 different ways
but poetic

not the page of notes from Ted Aoki
spidery black handwriting
should be donated to a memorial somewhere

not the writing that Carl inspired
not Carl's responses in the margins

once before I even met Carl
I saw him
a shadowy figure
in a long black coat
long hair
down a long university corridor
not your usual professor
more like a figure
from a PBS Masterpiece series

the world shifted that day
theses were gloriously poetic
dissertations broke boundaries
nothing was the same again
and song and poetry could be heard
in the echoes

Pondering the Ponderosa Pine

My work is rooted in silence.
It grows out of deep beds
of contemplation, where words, Pondering
which are living things,
can form and re-form
into new wholes.
(Jeanette Winterson)

for more than twenty-five years you have greeted me
on treks to Scarfe for meetings and more meetings,
or seeking coffee, the high-octane fuel of scholars,
or sitting in your shade, sipping coffee, pondering
if I really need to attend another meeting

I will not render you a metaphor
        in this poem
I will not anthropomorphize you
        like a Disney cartoon
I will not sentimentalize your saga of survival
        from weather, pests, and chainsaws
I will not pretend hermeneutically
        I know your essence
I will not claim I can name
        your existence in

        post-structuralist
                post-materialist
                        post-human
                                post-modern
                                        post-feminist
                                                post-colonialist

discourses, enough posts to build a fence around Ben Cartwright's Ponderosa

your wildness cannot be contained in my poem
any more than I can hold the moon's fullness in a pail

ever green, ever rooted, ever patient,
ever willing to teach us if we are willing to learn

teach us to remember we are guests
on an ancient land with countless stories

teach us to walk tenderly with one another,
filled with memories and hopes for others, too

teach us to know this place of mind
is also a place of mindfulness

in these last years I have at UBC
I will loiter often with you, and even if
I write fewer poems or papers, I might
yet learn to live like a scholar who knows
learning always begins with lingering

we no longer dwell in an annex
like an appendix or supplement

we will not pine for the Ponderosa Annexes
as we settle into the Ponderosa Commons

let us now dance an Argentinian tango
with light and shadow, with the rhythms
of the seasons, with the ebb and flow
of students and colleagues as we compose
new stories with the alphabet's possibilities,
new stories rooted in memory and imagination

Women's Labour

when I retired
years of service
teacher professor consultant
mother
(you can't retire from that)
every gold and red September
that sense of expectation
hope possibility

retire is a strange word
think of treads
mine are definitely worn

I had never been
out of school
grade school student to PhD
I have learned the wor(l)d
through the lens
of institutions

that's a lot of tires

I felt joy
freedom, a sense of release
and yet...
like a prisoner
who wants structure
longs for flight too
was conflicted
worried about letting go
what had held me aloft
for so long

all-weather tires deflate too

would the long days to September
be one blur of wavy radiant heat?
each day followed
by the next
no usual countdown
time, that trickster
seemingly endless time

air wooshes out

nothing is forever
my legacy of labour
will be forgotten
another cobweb hanging
on the tiled wall
who we were
what we did
why it mattered
tentative
easily blown away

something must remain
even air

What I did on my summer vacation
or
What I didn't do on my summer vacation
or
What I wish I had done on my summer vacation
or
What my Facebook friends (apparently) did on their summer vacation

(a poem in search of a title)
or
(a title in search of a poem)

though everything I write is nothing more than an allegory
emblem fragment gasp metaphor parable similitude
I still continue to write, even with hope

this summer, I (the real deal me,
not the lyrical I, the personified voice
of this rambling poem)
attended 40 meetings
assessed 31 portfolios
read 16 master's papers
responded to 15 submissions for a book
edited 12 articles for a journal issue
wrote 10 reference letters
reviewed 7 dissertation drafts
judged 6 AERA proposals and journal submissions
penned blurbs for 2 colleagues' book manuscripts
Skyped, phoned, and texted countless colleagues,
commuted, Cyborg-like, in the summer maze of Vancouver road construction,
and gobbled up e-mail messages like a ravenous Pac-Man
with an indomitable will to thrive amidst the *EEEEE* in e-mail
like the eerie scratch of a teacher's fingernails on an ancient blackboard

I did not dilly dally but diligently daily drove
the daunting dragon of desire and demand

while my Facebook friends {apparently}
did push-ups, ran effortless marathons, hiked tangled trails,

displayed tight, defined, ripped abs, not theirs, usually Bieber's,
waterskied, scuba-dived, skateboarded, biked, hiked, bowled,
painted their fingernails, picnicked, hung out, chilled, relaxed,
danced the salsa, drank beer, consumed photogenic lunches,
practiced karate and Karaoke and kayaking, rescued turkeys
and drowning horses, Trumped Trump with self-satisfied selfies,
expressed enough romance to make Nicholas Sparks blush,
made music, dyed their hair, got tattoos, and grew mustaches,
canoed and canoodled, cruised and chewed cashews,
some played horseshoes, a few even mentioned world news,
posted photos of puppies and pooches, celebrated births, birthdays,

engagements, weddings, even Facebook friendships as old as a year or so,
updated their profile images with daily diligence (I'm still using
the photo from over a decade ago because I will never look
that good again), laughed and laughed with lollygagging lunacy

I don't have a lot of Facebook friends, I don't even have a lot of friends
(a poet's occupational hazard), but my posse of friends visited
every country on the planet that begins with M, except Madagascar

my friends promoted intriguing books I know I will never read
(I can't keep up with Facebook—what chance do I have with books?),
found inner serenity, the sweet tangy taste of strawberry with beer,
10 essential gelato flavours, and 6 solutions for world peace,
not to mention aphorisms, maxims, and proverbs for loving living
(You might be given a cactus, but you don't have to sit on it.)

my Facebook friends smiled a lot, ate a lot, drank a lot,
laughed a lot, poked people, and pondered Pokemon,
posted images of Jesus in Portuguese buns, made
funny faces with false teeth, and composed the world
with the domestic nostalgia of Laura Ingalls Wilder

the one thing, the one thing none of my Facebook friends
did all summer was work—they were entirely idle,
indolent, languid, lethargic, lost in luxury and licentiousness

at 32 years old, Mark Zuckerberg
is the fifth richest person in the world
(probably stays up nights thinking about Bill and Warren)
every time one of my friends posts another image
of the sumptuous spaghetti and clams in olive oil and garlic
they are savouring on a summer patio in some exotic corner
of England Thailand Australia or Saskatchewan
Mark Zuckerberg marks another chunk of change
he claims he has more to give away

I don't know what to make of Zuckerberg, I am too busy
liking my friends' posts to attend creatively and critically
to Zuckerberg's vision and ambition, drive and desire

like Columbus Cortes Cabot Cook Cartier Coronado
Zuckerberg confesses, "The thing I really care about is
the mission, making the world open"
the mission, making the world open

in August I visited my mother in Newfoundland
if I had posted images of my mother,
I would have smiled, she probably
would have smiled too, though
she doesn't like smiling for a camera,
and if I had posted such a photo
you would never guess how the hours
I spent with my mother this summer
were mostly spent wondering, who
is this woman I have known for more
than 62 years and still don't know?

the son's sad sense of persistent befuddlement
cannot be expressed on Facebook
where the facetious reigns, where
faces are rendered glamourously
with Hollywood's superficial gloss and alchemy,
an aging son's lingering angst is no story for Facebook

or I could write about Terry, my childhood friend,
who died with a stroke or an aneurysm, not sure,
or Paul who died with ALS, all too sure,
or Uncle Bud who wonders if bungee jumping
might have caused his creeping dementia

I could tell you many stories that broke my heart
in the month of August alone, but those stories
will remain unspoken—who can receive them—
an old man's sadness is best hidden
like yellow toenails and wrinkled body parts
not even old men can think about

Mark Zuckerberg is the only one of my friends
who wants me to be open but since Mark Z. is
not really my bud, I will continue to eye Facebook
with suspicion and author only the stories authorized by

Butler's performativity
        Baudrillard's hyperreality
Cixous' dreams
        Deleuze's rhizomes
Haraway's posthumanism
        Derrida's différance
Irigaray's mimesis
        Foucault's panopticon
Kristeva's semiotic
        Levinas' ethics
Sedgwick's neologisms
        Barthes' mythologies

(so glad I can write wonderful gibberish
to confound Facebook friends wallowing in
their images of animal antics and foodie passions?)

in a poetic spell of word-making
where language will not languish
in the anguish of APA authority

I continue to embrace

alphabetic adventures
biophilic biography
coherent composition
dramatic denotation
energetic errors
fecund fictions
gregarious grammar
haunting holiness
incendiary idiolect
joyful journaling
kinetic knowledge
ludic language
meandering murmurations
noumenal narration
organic orations
poetic playfulness
questing questions
ruminative representation
sensual savouring
textual truth
urgent ululation
vibrant verbs
whimsical witnessing
xylophonic xerography
yearning yammering
zestful zeugmas

What did I do on my summer vacation?

this summer, I (the real deal me,
not the lyrical I, the personified voice
of this rambling poem)
attended 40 meetings
assessed 31 portfolios
read 16 master's papers

responded to 15 submissions for a book
edited 12 articles for a journal issue
wrote 10 reference letters
reviewed 7 dissertation drafts
judged 6 AERA proposals and journal submissions
penned blurbs for 2 colleagues' book manuscripts
Skyped, phoned, and texted countless colleagues,
commuted, Cyborg-like, in the summer maze of Vancouver road construction
and gobbled up e-mail messages like a ravenous Pac-Man
with an indomitable will to thrive amidst the *EEEEE* in e-mail
like the eerie scratch of a teacher's fingernails on an ancient blackboard

I did not dilly dally but diligently daily drove
the daunting dragon of desire and demand

and I wrote this poem

all that remains is the obligatory
selfie of the poet reading his poem
for posting to Facebook

Empty Nest #2

some flew back
to the nest
such a short time
alone

circumstances these days
mean young adults move back
with the old
common support offered:
job loss, high rents,
more university

blessed to have had
extra time with daughters
no Empty Nest Syndrome for this Mama Bird

but now I spread my wings
soar over daughters' new nests
swooping my approval
content they are moving forward
so I, too, can fly

once I wrote
how I'd miss the noise
& I did
then did not
relish the freedom
space to hear my own thoughts

Queen of the nest once more
no longer warming it
standing guard a different way
taking flight
me, Renee, flying

Cancer (on) Ward

in July I was diagnosed with
Diffuse Large B Cell Lymphoma
which at least sings with poetic rhythms

I am now sipping a hot chocolate
in the BC Cancer Agency

I have joined the circle of the elderly,
    perhaps prematurely,
while I wait patiently, a patient patient

Lymphoma Canada claims DLBCL
responds well to treatment with a high rate of cure

I am now cancer, pervasive, everywhere,
flowing blood cells, normal and abnormal,
I am aswirl with blood cancer

cancer is the uninvited guest you do not
want but do not know how to refuse,
a spectre who haunts every moment
like a noxious scent sent from far away

I am now Carl with Cancer, a character,
    illness journey   illness story
    illness trajectory   illness adventure

I just drank a Marble Slab Creamery
strawberry milkshake, satisfied

regarding cancer, constipation,
consternation, I want conversation

will I get porridge in the morning?
French fries are coming for lunch

Lana in a white summer dress
ready for the Mayan Riviera or here

the nurses are generous
like elementary school teachers

I have received many texts and prayers
and love notes, glad and guilty,
when did I become so popular?

rather odd to arrive at a place
    where I am almost content
        how does that happen?
            how do we become happy?

time moves slowly
    just like always

I miss my granddaughters flowing
with stories to be written and lived

I fell this morning, crumpled supine
on the floor, TC gave me a walker

Lana and I lie on the narrow bed,
play Scrabble and Yahtzee

Peter and his wife chat behind their curtain,
    Peter coughs, his wife whispers

carpenters cleaners clerks cooks
counsellors diagnosticians doctors
educators electricians managers
nurses pharmacists plumbers
providers specialists technicians

machinery beeps   purrs   alerts
a barrage of memos regarding healing
    processes and possibilities

coming and going
    murmuring and mumbling

any nausea? bowel movements?

why are salmon pink curtains
    popular in hospitals?

my granddaughters are faraway, now on
their own adventures where I cannot join them,
I love them, and I hold them fast in the light
of the heart, but they are on their journeys,
and I am mostly absent, holed up in a hospital

I am very tired today, just slept
at least an hour this afternoon

second round of chemo, platelets too low
to begin on Wednesday, so we went home
and returned on Thursday when I had
one platelet more than the minimum,
and it is now Saturday afternoon and
the chemo transfusions should be over
by about 8pm tonight, and I will rest

in the Agency on Sunday and hopefully
be discharged on Monday or Tuesday

I must continue to learn to flow with the story
that unfolds, I really know nothing, each day
composes a story and I learn from the story
(I hope I can learn what I need to know)

I pee at least every hour
    I pee a lot
I am learning the familiar rhythm

Lana is doing a crossword puzzle
or knitting or sending messages to family

enjoyed coffee and a berry scone
    at Elysian

good news today! Dr. Sehn told us
    the chemo is working
and the tumour is much diminished
and she used several modifiers
I can't remember, but they were all
filled with confident encouragement
and I am beginning to relax
with the hope that I might really
have some more time left
to work and play and enjoy family

on the cancer ward I am tethered
to tubes transfusion bags monitors
which I drag here and there
on a kind of coat rack on wheels

the woman in charge of the kitchen
is from Fiji and remembers the brown sugar
she mixed with oatmeal as a child

my metatrexate level is 0.09
(happily below the level it must be)

I am especially eager
for some physical exercise

Disneyland, here we come!

in the BC Cancer Agency we all have cancer
    and every cancer is different,
written with fear and hope

we all have stories on the cancer ward
and all our stories are different,
especially when they are really the same

Researching Death

I am researching
how to transport dead bodies
specifically my mother
who's not actually dead yet
worry someone will think
I'm planning murder

I am researching
whether air carriers
transport dead bodies
from one city to another
specifically my mother
in a Vancouver old age home
to a Calgary cemetery
beside my father
who is actually dead
I long to put a stone
on his grave

my sister conveys
my mother's wishes
at our holiday dinner
amongst friends and a turkey
who is also dead

we grieve our mother's
accelerating descent into dementia
masked by comic macabre

my sister wants
to be prepared
our mother is 89
there's not going to be
any miracles here
no oil burning
for 89 days or nights
no Maccabees to fight
the battle of Alzheimer's

when I hear
the estimated cost
I say I'll drive her
one last trip to Calgary
like the grandpa
in Little Miss Sunshine
our lawyer relatives
remind us of legalities
dark humour aside

my sister
serious for a moment
looks me in the eye
will I come with her
to Calgary
bury our mother
beside our father
throw a handful of dirt on the grave

I agree
we have already been mourning
a mind lost
language gone,
the body last to go

our daughters murmur
they will come too
this and my sister's eyes
travel straight to my depths
no monetary cost
but oh,
so much currency spent

I am researching
how to transport
a dead body
write down quotes
remember the Talmudic words
in the hall
when I visit my mother:
"Do not cast me off in old age..."

a stone for the graves

Scarlet A

the Canadian Carcass Poultry Grading Program
offers three grades:

> *Canada A grade*
> *Canada Utility grade*
> *Canada C grade*

I have been in school more than
sixty years, as a student or a teacher

I learned in the beginning how to be
a good student, and now close

to retirement after a lifetime
of being a student and a teacher

I am still learning to be good
I am on medical leave while

I receive extensive treatment for cancer,
I miss teaching, I miss the classroom

I miss talking with colleagues
about the joys and challenges of teaching

I might never return to teaching
I might need to retire, or I might

simply wave good-bye to the whole
complex, jumbled experience of being

human, and pass on to whatever lies
beyond this—always hoping

I have spent my life seeking A's—why?
why is A prioritised? as a Christian

I anticipate heaven, and really whether
or not there is a heaven, all that matters

to me right now is the idea that I might
soon wake up in a consciousness

or place or livelihood or existence
where I will know that the old life

is done and a new life has begun
or I might not wake up at all

assuming there is a heaven, an after life,
an eternal life, a life with God,

then what will be the value of all
the A's on all the report cards

I have received? should I get
my CV tattooed on my body

so I might somehow carry it with me,
will God want to see my CV?

will I want to show it to anybody?
how do I live in this world

as a hopeful testimony to life after this world?
what is my value? Canada A grade chicken?

Letting Go

I am not ready to let her go. Not when she still giggles when I tell her I love her, tell her she is the best mother in the whole world. No, she doesn't giggle every time. Sometimes she has collected spit in her mouth and she won't swallow. I tell her I love her on spitball days, but she doesn't respond except with a closed-mouth grunt. Who's to say that isn't some kind of acknowledgment, some kind of visceral connection to love, even if it's not articulate? When language is lost, does kinship disappear?

Sometimes she dozes, so I hold her hand. She hates when my hands are cold, so then I rub her back, make physical contact so she feels my presence. My husband comes with me on our visits. We are both sad she is in a wheelchair, is in the throes of dementia, is but a ghost of her former self. Sad that on every visit we confront our own mortality.

In the hall of the home where my mother resides, there is a quote from the Hebrew Book of Psalms: "Do not cast me off in old age; When my strength fails, do not forsake me." When I first walked by this psalm, I stopped and wrote it down. It spoke to me as a poet, as a loving daughter, as the loving mother of daughters.

Look, Mom, I say. Don, my husband is here. Out of the blue one day she responded: You're a good boy! She still eats, even though her food is soft, and rarely refuses the ice cream I like to feed her because I know it is a favourite. And I remember her telling me about her father, who lived to 95. "He eats well, he still wants to eat," she commented, after visits to the nursing home where she and her sisters took turns spoon feeding him. "That's what keeps him going," my mother said. I never once heard her wish he would die. She visited him and fed him and then did it all over again, out of love, out of duty, out of gratitude.

Yesterday I learned a poet acquaintance with whom I attended graduate school died of cancer at 59. She suffered for four years, continuing to write, and a final poem she wrote to her daughter broke my heart. She stayed on this earth until her last breath. It's all so complicated, life and death and dignity. My poet acquaintance fought until the end. My mother is not capable of making decisions. How can we know what she wants? How can we know that she is ready to die? Are there unconscious and complex heart-to-heart impulses which we know nothing about that keep her here on earth? I am not ready to let my mother go. So I will continue to visit her, out of love, out of duty, out of gratitude..

The Pen

(for Rick)

years ago, when my first book of poems
Growing Up Perpendicular on the Side of a Hill
was published, my brother sent me
a silver Cross pen with my name engraved

my brother sometimes complained
I made money by writing poetry

about his mishaps and calamities (I always
explained, poets don't make any money)

a year ago, I lost the pen, and while I lose
a lot of pens, I was especially sad to lose
the pen my brother had given me, a gesture
he was glad I wrote stories, even his

on the eve of my birthday I was culling
clothes in my closet (a seasonal purging
to sustain balance amidst busy clutter)
with hope that the Thrift Store had room

I found the pen in the pocket of a winter jacket,
and remembered how my brother always
phoned me on my birthday with the boast,
I'm now two years younger than you, at least

for a week, since he was born one year
and one week after me, always my best friend
growing up on Lynch's Lane, and for all our
differences, he was the brother I always needed

since he died last August, he will always be much
younger now, and finding the lost pen I knew
how a lovely mystery holds us fast, even in loss,
when my brother whispered, *write more poems*

57th and Oak

how those girls must have dreamed
soaring above their bodies
the stranger growing in their womb
a constant reminder
shame, regret, pain
the hallmarks of decency
hydrangeas and sturdy oaks
surrounding this house of reluctant mothers
this intersection of broken beginnings

and now my mother mindless
plucks a flower as she walks the path
along this same house transformed
rooms full of strangers
this house of lost memory
this place of endings
this sad intersection

Algebra

(for Lana)

love is enough heartbreak to fill
a season of *Coronation Street*

love is fictions fragments figments fractures
fired in the heart's foundry

love is Madeleine in her Oscar costume
wearing the dress you wore on our honeymoon

love is knowing the creation is always creating
with the creator's collaboration

love is leaning into the wind, hauling hard
on the line that does not break

love is the geometry of the Steveston winter sky
trusting in a fundamental theorem

love is Mirabelle on roller skates
remembering our first date

love is saying good-bye to family and friends
moving from one ocean to another, new stories

love is getting it wrong much of the time
but still shaping a right angle in complements

love is seeking the divine and ineffable amidst
the distinctly human, even in the inevitable wounds

love is Gwenoviere, arms stretched out
for the whole world like we knew long ago

love is Yahtzee Monopoly Scrabble where
so much depends on who gets X

love is caressing a scar, a reminder
of what was and might have been

love is living on borrowed money and hope
remembering heartbreak with forgiveness

love is Alexandria, wearing wigs and costumes
like her father always wore, filled with make-believe

love is learning to live alongside the stranger
the inscrutable and intimate other

love is iterable irritable inimitable illimitable
inhabitable irresistible irascible inflamed

love is algebra (Arabic, *al-jabr*), like our story
the reunion of broken parts

I.

Grandmother at Last

I am waiting
excited, tense
are the babies delivered?
and finally
their father texts
from the delivery room
millennial messaging
mother and twins doing well

at the hospital
my husband, machetunem, and I
wait
at last we are allowed entry
the postpartum room
two baby girls
an A on one hat, a B on the other
in my daughter's arms
I look at her
we both cry

I hold the babies
one by one
hello Frances
hello June
softly sing to them
rock and hug
a grandmother at last
the smell of miracle
wonder
in the air
my heart astir

II.

Franny, Franny, Franny, You're a Double Whammy

I hold you Frances
sing you lullabies
have been brushing up
for months
as you rocked with June
in your mother's womb

you look up at me
that sweet small face
mirror image of June
your innocence
open to this new world
of smells, sounds,
your mother's milk

your eyes flutter
open again
shut with the sway
of my arms
the singsong of melodies

warming you
loving you
welcoming you
remembering distant joy

III.

June, June, June, Flying to the Moon

and you, June
twin poems for baby girls
a scratch
on your newly formed forehead
distinguishes you

you mewl
cry for mother's breast
but we must wait for now
so I rock you too
sing more lullabies:
cradles, hush you bye,
don't you cry
I'll catch that cradle
in the wind
and you too
before a fall

you suck your fingers
root for my breast
as empty now
as my heart is full

and you, June
mirror image of Frances
settle into my warmth

Patio Ruminations

the early evening light
in my neighbour's cedar
invites me to be still

still I am compelled
to tweet these words
a sole survivor's SOS

under a moon, almost full,
I am learning to listen
for cherry blossoms
like a new alphabet
for calling out love

Saturday spring sunshine
in Steveston with seagulls
seeking summer's stories
like scents on the skin

poetry happens
in moments when
you are attending
to what is there
and not there,
when rhythms
of light and shadow
animate imagination

Sunday on the patio
in sunlight stepping
through clouds, still
eager to embrace
more than meets
even esoteric tweets,
always hopeful, full

instead of a table of contents
my life story begins with
a table of contentments:
long lasting love, a cursive
script from there to here

on a sunlit Sunday
at the playground
with granddaughters
I lean into the autumn
light with a poet's
hope for all of us

what would happen if
all the poets in all the world
suddenly disappeared,
grew silent, lost their voices?

October light, still,
holds fast poems
fired in summer,
in case winter's sun
forgets its point
inscribes a circle,
always hope full

In Osoyoos

among the ashes
a smoke of fog
surrounds the mountains
cactus dry
the sun breaking through
early morning in this desert

no sooner do I get arranged
on my chaise lounge
time to move
out of sun's searing rays

no easy task these days
hips, back, neck
what fresh hell is this?
I ask
some metal parts
the disability of inability
to turn my head
turn away
from the sun
from whatever comes our way

I ice my way
through nights and days
content my family around me
adult children grown
but still connected

and it's fine
good to leave the stress
work, daily lives
lift ourselves to the sun
even ash
water,
playful games
laughter

this is when
the Phoenix rises
when the tenuous
overstretched cords of connection
fuse
and bonding rebuilds

I lift my degenerating neck
to the warmth of summer sun
pain the alternative
to a much more final end

fire burns through
much more than grass, forests
the falling ash a snowfall
of remembrance

if I lie here long enough
will I too be covered
with gray flakes of regret
those harsh words
that cranky morning
that emotional outburst
all forgotten
or is it?

underneath a dusting:
burned brush, scorched earth
like getting rid of trees
infested with pine needles
peace resurrected
new growth in the future

A Poem Is

a heart beat   a light breath

a dream hanging on the line

stretched between poles we cannot see

falling in love with the alphabet

growing intimate with grammar and syntax

a game of peek-a-boo   scribbles in snow

a call, filled with hope somebody will hear

a message in a bottle dropped in the sea

attending to the familiar with unfamiliar words

a love note sent to creatures light years away

words infused with the heart's rhythms

words, efficacious, capacious, effervescent words

enjoying the sunlight through the study blinds

learning to live attentively in tentative times

cedars dancing in my neighbor's backyard

Poet's Symphony

above the words
the turns of the flute
under the saxophone trills
in the spaces between the keys
but the letters will not behave

up and down the scale
they turn and lift
lift and thrust
dancing on the ascent
descending into the chaos
of chorus

dry reeds crack
words burn holes
pads come loose
POP!
the sound is an earthquake of alphabet
silent as a deaf mute
raging
hands signing thoughts

it is enough to play
the words

DEATH WATCH

Once taut, steeled with wise words,
I am broken, empty, full of fear,
like living in a radioactive zone after a spill
Carl Leggo

Walking a Tightrope

(November 6, 2018)

while Americans vote
in the mid-terms, with the world
    suspended on the invisible
    wires of lunacy and lies,
I plan for a medical appointment
with Dr. Sehn, my oncologist

  if the news is bad

I will cuddle my granddaughters
      I will sit on the patio with Lana
I will drink a martini with Lana
      I will write a poem for Lana
I will see a film with Aaron
      I will go to lunch with Anna
I will retire
      I will clean out my office
I will contact graduate students
      I will consult with the Head and Dean
I will update family
      I will inform the Department and Faculty
I will quit Facebook
      I will rehearse NO
I will sort out pensions
      I will plan a party for family
I will give away personal stuff, if anybody wants it
      I will visit O'Hare's Pub
I will walk on the dike near the Fraser River

if the news is good

I will cuddle my granddaughters
I will sit on the patio with Lana
I will drink a martini with Lana
I will write a poem for Lana
I will see a film with Aaron
I will go to lunch with Anna
I will retire
I will clean out my office
I will contact graduate students
I will consult with the Head and Dean
I will update family

I will inform the Department and Faculty
I will quit Facebook
I will sort out pensions
I will plan a party for family
I will give away personal stuff, if anybody wants it
I will visit O'Hare's Pub
I will walk on the dike near the Fraser River

while Americans vote
in the mid-terms, with the world
suspended on the invisible
wires of lunacy and lies,
I plan for a medical appointment
with Dr. Sehn, my oncologist

Signs of Spring

I stop reading the obituaries
temporarily
delete emails in my inbox
clean out 20 plus years
of old toys and school papers
the rattle of the coughing man across the creek
can be heard more often now

I check employment opportunities
a habit difficult to break
walk the dog
whose pace now matches mine
keep old birthday cards
from my mother to my daughters
there is no catch in the coughing man's coughs
across the creek

I dig out capris to wear
don't bother to shave my legs
rejoice at Easter once again
I don't have to hide chocolate eggs
keep daughters' cat sketches & potion recipes
the coughing man across the creek
fights for breath

Spring air full of remembrance
regret:
death's pollen

What Does Love Taste Like?

I have never seen a tree struck by lightning
the flare of gold light swallowing a century or so
of patient growing and waiting with expectation

I have never heard the rain fall so long and hard
the river cannot contain the bounty and spills
into lanes and basements, unwanted destruction

I have never tasted dust laced with carcinogens
like my friend's father breathed in the cement plant
daily until cancer killed him, another statistic

I have never smelled the ash after a house fire
when wood, linoleum, enamel, flesh are all
incinerated with intense and wild indifference

I have never touched God's face, have seldom
known the touch of others either, like I am
cast out into the darkness, Gehenna even

but I have sat beside a bed in palliative care
where my brother with thin skin stretched
over his skull and shoulders breathed shallow

and death was toxic with relentless drive
while I touched my brother for the first time
in many years, for the last time, tasted love

Death Watch

I am not supposed to write
about the night my daughters
kept vigil over my dying mother
so she was not alone

this is my poem to write,
a daughter says
a bit of warning in her voice

so I will write
about love, sacrifice
about mothers & daughters
how my heart was breaking
as my mother rasped
into the oxygen mask

how my daughters arrived & cried
then again days later
at the cemetery in Calgary
my mother lowered into the earth
beside my father
we shovelled dirt 3 times each
daughters rubbing my shoulders
crying
so that I didn't know
where my dirt, my tears
ended & theirs began
or is it the other way round?

we could laugh too
in the motel room at 3 AM
all farting one at a time

the march of the trumpets, I said
the bumpets, Don said
air on a G string, you said
the daughter who won't let me write
about the vigil
their mitzvah, their good deed
but I'm giving you credit
and it's a good title for a fart fest

and although I'm not supposed
to write about that night
I'm going to tell
how you told me
you each held her hand
as she took her last breaths

how (exhausted) you begged
to come home
but stayed
guarding your bubby's body
Jewish tradition
until my sisters came

I can tell how heroic you are
how brave & strong & true
how loving
performing this mitzvah
in tribute

I can write how I love
the young women you have become
how blessed I am
you are in my life
how I know my passage
will be brighter
because of you

If I Knew I Was Dying

if I knew I was dying, I would write a poem
for Lana and tell her she is beautiful

if I knew I was dying, I would write poems for Anna and Aaron
and for Madeleine and Mirabelle and Gwenoviere and Alexandria

if I knew I was dying, I would not read any more books
and focus instead on remembering all the books I have not read

if I knew I was dying, I would watch *Doctor Zhivago* again,
no movie has ever captivated me like *Doctor Zhivago*

if I knew I was dying, I would hike a favourite trail
in Newfoundland or British Columbia

if I knew I was dying, I would eat a jumbo fries
at New York Fries (with gravy and malt vinegar and salt)

if I knew I was dying, I would clean out my office at UBC
and hope the next occupant will enjoy it as I have enjoyed it

if I knew I was dying, I would send notes to a circle of friends
and colleagues to wish them well in their life journeys

if I knew I was dying, I would sit quietly
and let God fill my imagination with prayers

if I knew I was dying, I wouldn't watch much TV
or read internet stories about Donald Trump

if I knew I was dying, I would drink
pinot noir and gin martinis, every evening

if I knew I was dying, I would listen to a lot of music,
especially Leonard Cohen and Willie Nelson

if I knew I was dying, I would go to bed early
and wake up late

if I knew I was dying, I would go to the Cactus Club
and order the Rob Feenie-inspired barbequed duck club sandwich

if I knew I was dying, I would enjoy
a bath every day with Avon *Skin So Soft*
if I knew I was dying, I would look forward to life
after death, the eternal journey, the heavenly life

if I knew I was dying, I would sit on the patio
with Lana and hold her hand and tell her I love her

if I knew I was dying, I would stop
writing this poem

Notes for My Daughters in the Event I Develop Dementia

feed me ice cream
lots of it
you know my favourite
visit me
you'll feel better
I know it's sad
I'm sad about your Bubby

don't assist my dying
I want to be there
viscerally connected
reluctant to leave you

know I love you
always
joy of my life
nothing I accomplished
compares

forgive my mistakes
you will make some too
human I rate myself
far from perfect

if I lose language like Bubby
every movement
every facial tic
every blink of an eye
me telegraphing our connection

when you return
to your homes families
think of me
not as a burden
though it will be one
think of me as your champion
your good luck charm
your best friend
think beyond my silence
your greatest supporter

the blank look in my eyes
every slant of sun or shade
mark our years together
not even this decay
can fracture that

Learning to Swim

cut clover, startled sun, fast cold stream
dammed to create an oblong swimming pool

how many summers did my brother and I
spend at Margaret Bowater Park

on clear blue days when it never rained
and languorous afternoons unfolded

with the patience of the grass at the base
of the old rock where we pretended

we were Tarzan plunging into the Congo
to fight yet another crocodile, the only

thing we knew about crocodiles, wrestling,
avoiding their jaws and teeth, sticking

the knife in, not always easy to carry
a sharp knife around your naked waist

but Johnny Weissmuller could, so we
carried sticks in a loop of string and bore

the occasional scratches with fortitude
always sure a few new wounds proclaimed

our brave singular adventures like
the lifeguard's whistle warning us

to stay away, get down, come back
from all the places we weren't allowed

all the places that seduced our imaginations
with perils and pearls, hardy and hearty

stories full of trembling and tumbling
a long time ago, still present, now

my brother, the bravest, toughest,
strongest swimmer of us all

did we have a half dozen summers?
we couldn't swim when we started

every early July our skin burned red
peeled, turned brown and freckled

at least a half dozen summers tuned
in tones, mottled jumbled tangled

packed with enough stories to tax an abacus
a lifetime, now my brother is dead

and I am here alone, like visiting
a cemetery except there are families

children teens all enjoying the park
as we once enjoyed it, eventually

became lifeguards and swam competitively
with the Corner Brook Rapids Swim Club

my brother won the second place ribbon
for the 200 meter butterfly at the provincial meet

once upon a time in a universe far away without end
my brother climbed the arch over the dam

defied the lifeguard's strident whistle and flew
into the air so high even the wind stopped racing him

Rhubarb Remembrance

I'm making your rhubarb pie, Mom
as the flame on my mourner's candle
flickers, glows
I imagine you are responding

my dough is a mess
I have to patch it together
like I'm using play dough

I can hear you
the non-demented you
WHAT THE HELL DID YOU DO?

in my defence
I used whole wheat flour
I'm grieving
my eyes are red-veined

the recipe
is in your neat handwriting
back before you lost language
when my daughters were younger
remember
when Don came to Calgary?
he'd never had rhubarb pie
at first he refused
but he loves that pie
it's his favourite now
I HOPE HE DOESN'T MIND
YOUR WHOLE WHEAT CRUST

I'm serving this pie
to my machetunem
they gave me the rhubarb
it's what I know
you would have done
your dough would have been perfect
but you would not have used
whole wheat flour
I hope they don't mind the crust

you are here with me
you are in me

London Farm

(October 13, 2018)

almost three months
after the diagnosis
of a brain tumour

on this Saturday
with a blue sky
of autumn promise

I joined Lana and Anna
for the fall clean-up
at London Farm where

we share a garden plot
though I didn't plan
to join them but realized

I needed to be
outdoors with others,
even working

I tore down a fence
with Egon who is old enough
to recall building the fence

and now I am sitting
on a bench, sipping
water, watching everyone

else, dreaming about
being more robust,
savouring the moment

when I look up and see
an eagle floating
like eagles have sailed

here for more than
a century and will
linger for many more

Slugs I

I hunt through the grass
pouring salt wounds
on slugs
I was not always
the salt murderer
at first kind
tossing them in the creek

by the third planting
it gets personal:
tiny new spinach leaves,
feathery carrot tops gone,
radishes with one bite missing

a slug even crept
up the tomato pot
the nerve!

just in case I have the wrong culprits
I fashion a makeshift scarecrow
with Hallowe'en decorations
witch on a broom,
skeletons on poles
birds beware!
embarrassed
my daughter begs me:
remove them

but I am the vigilant gardener now
a little OCD I check day and night
relate to Beatrix Potter's Mr. MacGregor
this garden will produce
or more slugs will die
trying...

still
I wonder
about the progress of slugs
that stinging coat of salt
the soft bed of creek

Slugs II

your slow movement
to my lettuce
a death watch
kills my gardening spirit

what?
you no longer bite bait
boldly crawl up my pot
of lettuce
snatch your route
to pest purgatory

I see your belly
baring my lovely leaves
this is salad slaughter
I mourn
miss the grilled green
lettuce livery
spring ensemble in tatters

After 40 Years, You

might expect 40 poems
each with 40 stanzas
composed in 40 lines

instead of this poem
cobbled together
in 40 quiet minutes

like a long breath
in the chaos of Las Vegas
where everybody is

somebody else, or
wants to be someplace
else, in other stories,

while you and I
celebrate long love
knowing this gift

is granted, not
taken for granted,
received gladly,

and while I have
scribbled this poem
in morning minutes

we have been revising
the poem for over
40 years, knowing how

the mystery of grammar
always holds us in process,
this story without end

how a life can hold
countless memories
in intimate moments

like neon lights in a Vegas
nightscape, defying all
simple interpretations

so all I know in this moment
expressed lightly in a poem
40 years in the making

is how in all of Las Vegas
with its memories of meadows
and tribute bands and magicians

Celine Dion and Elton John
Cirque de Soleil acrobatics
and casino promises of fortune

I know with joy our love story
defies illusions and delusions
rooted in the heart's measure

and lying on the pool deck
in the Vegas summer sun,
side by side, your pink bikini

reminds me this poem
is always full of surprises
like the story is just beginning

after 40 years, you
are the one who breathes
in this poem & all the poems

Writing Daughters

(for Erin)

she asks me
why that poem?
an older one I include in a manuscript
why do her sisters have newer poems?
I show her where she is
in my garden poem
other poems where she exists
between the lines
she is my baby
the one I rocked last
locked in memory
I wonder
am I avoiding
the young woman she's become?
or overlooking what's important

it's risky writing daughters
fraught with emotional politics
but I will write her here
all her gentleness, compassion
the way she perceives a situation
suggests advice I never thought of
her feminisms make me proud
she is open
quick to defend difference
her sense of responsibility
strong like her values
quiet she listens more than speaks
playful we call her the puppy
her quirky humour delights

I shaped clay
beside her at the pottery wheel
watched her long sensitive
artistic fingers
lift the clay
widen
add touches
a creativity
that took my breath away
like the clay
she transforms
no sculptor-mother I
she is both clay & artist
becoming more beautiful
as I write her

Sanctuary

most of my adult life I have spent Sundays
in church, but cancer has consumed my spirit,
so I now spend Sundays at the Sanctuary,
a coffee shop a few minutes up the road

Tim built the coffee shop, especially for cyclists,
where *Coffee Cycle Culture* is the slogan and highlights
of Tour de France races are presented on a big screen
hung over the coffee bar, a gathering place

for cycling groups from all over the Lower Mainland
who arrive in happy numbers in spandex and cleated
shoes with expensive bicycles and camaraderie
to drink coffee and eat raspberry and lemon scones

Tim remembers people's names, asks about their stories,
he knows I am now often in the BC Cancer Agency
and he is always glad to see me, glad to hear treatments
are working, I might actually have some future left

perhaps I will ride a bicycle again, one day, as I often did
in Corner Brook, and one Christmas bought a Raleigh
ten-speed and had it shipped by train across Newfoundland,
with anticipation of riding it in the spring after a long winter

I look forward to returning to church on Sunday mornings
but for now I will sip coffee at the Sanctuary where
I can relax in the predictable pleasures of cycles of stories
that continue week after week, a simple air of repetition

Painting with Your Tongue

what does it mean
when you see green and say orange?
that you're colour blind
the synapses in your pop server
are not connected
you were distracted by a fruit salad
that it was a Freudian peel
that your mind
was on the traffic in the right-hand lane
there is too much green anyway
 as a poet you took poetic license
that you can't drive, talk, and chew colour
at the same time
and anyway orange
is just a redder shade of green
that you were painting with your tongue
you were talking with crayola
viewing the world through orange-coloured glasses
that you are losing your mind
losing your vision
losing words
losing green
trying to get everyone to take notice
orange doesn't get its due
and after all, who decided green is green
and at least you realized what you'd said
at the red light
when you stopped screaming

Bent

... voices ought not be measured by how pretty they are.
Instead they matter only if they convince you
... they are telling the truth.
Sam Cooke

a poem is a heart's beat

poetic light
bent around
the heart's
opaque hope
for a story
steeped in love

a poem is a message in a bottle afloat in the sea

an old man's skin
is like newsprint used
for fish and chips
and obituaries

a poem is a light breath

we live in wild words
loved, but wary still,
never weary, vigilant
in the tangles
the poet knows
are charmed with
the Trickster's breath

a poem is infused with the heart's rhythms

an open poem   an open palm
she slapped me with an open poem

a poem is scribbles in snow

amidst sun-infused memories
of January I still hope
for glimpses of return

a poem is a clothesline of words dancing in the wind

the clothesline, parallel lines
in a MacLean's notebook
I once wrote letters in
rehearsed scribbles
a crow signs light
with cursive precision
a story unfolds

a poem is a game of peek-a-boo

I wander
  with hums
Winnie the Pooh
  says poetry
happens
  when you let
hums come in

a poem is in love with the alphabet

in March in Newfoundland
I fall in love with winter's
unwavering hope for spring

a poem is capacious and efficacious

I wait
  arms open

the rain falls
  each drop a poem

a poem is a love note from faraway

writing poetry is like barbecuing
    you listen to the gulls
    watch your neighbours
    breathe slowly
    trust intuition to spell
        DONE

a poem is a dream hanging on the line

Newfoundland in March
is all blank pages and lines
a black and white world

longing for poems

a poem is underwear on a clothesline

stomach growls
like bullfrogs
in a slough

a poem is a call, somebody might hear

seeking serenity
in the midst of this and that
I will never know
the crew who blow
the autumn leaves
outside my office
window, traces lost

a poem is lingering sabbatically in words

on this solstice day, full of light,
I read Seamus Heaney, and note
how I am still present in all
the places I have lingered

a poem is spring sunlight to be savoured

where do words begin
where do words go
where are words when
they are in between

a poem is the heart tuned tight so it twangs

to know the whole story
    you must
know the hole in the story

a poem is skating the smooth page under a full moon

I am a fragment
my story is fragments

fragments will hold
the light long enough

to see the way round
the next curve

a poem is hearing the heart's light vibrate

in my poetry I always
have an appointment
with disappointment

a poem is intimate with syntax

the Sabbath is
an ancient poetic rhythm
as old as creation

The Poetics of Politics

if I were a politician
I would...
hold debates on words like affect and effect
mail out my poems on flyers
put one billion dollars into the infrastructure of stanzas
build pipelines of poems
announce free trade agreements on adjectives
decry the poverty of poetry
hammer signs with poems into the ground
in public places

I would...
conduct a poll on the last poetry book
my opponents read or bought
hell, the last poem they even read
hold rallies where speakers read poems
to the crowd
organize fundraisers to collect donations
for the arts
door knock in neighbourhoods
and read my poems to families on doorsteps

I would...
run ads in newspapers that showcased poets and poems
start a run for rhythm
a walk for words
a vote for verse

if I were a politician

Burma-shave

Heavy Work

In your poetry language is doing the heavy work.
(anonymous reviewer)

a
deciding what to leave
        in   heavy work

b
belonging   longing to be

c
instead of being in opposition
I want to be in apposition

d
there is no prize in surprise

e
what happened   happened

f
fun fundament   fundamentalism
forgets the fundament of fun

g
untangling the knot in monotony   metonymy

h
how are you?   well   you?
well   I think
not sure?   not really
not really?   a real knot

i
my calling is to love words
in their mystery

j
a poem is wild with longing
the longing for light
and night

k
I want to live
in the world
like a word
that lives love

l
angry with acronyms: IT, cIRcle, FGPS FSC
acrimonious acronyms arousing arachnophobia

m
morning   mourning   moaning   Monday moaning

n
  aesthetic
writing life into meaning
  an/aesthetic
writing meaning into life

o
if I write on this page without ink,
am I writing? can I think without ink?

p
I carry my working class baggage
like a turtle shell
   Sisyphus' rock
a hoarder's U-Haul

q
I have wrapped myself in a quilt of guilt

r
consumed, but not defined
by regrets   still
leaning into each day's hope

s
it was a dark and stormy
morning   all the difference

t
is life a run-on sentence?

u
when I receive a speeding ticket,
I include it in my CV as a citation

v
my daily planner fills up faster
than a Newfoundland backyard
in a November snowstorm

w
delusions of both
gravity and levity

x
after his wife Ruth died, a neighbour said,
he is now ruthless

y
yearning for learning
yearning for you   your yearning
learning with yearning

z
deciding what to leave
        out   heavy work

LOOK UP, UP, UP

breathe in   out   again
hear the entire world from there
the heart's steady rhythm
Carl Leggo

Manning Park, Lightning Lake

(for Don)

on the way home
from Osoyoos
sitting in the car
first reading, then writing
then watching
Don fishes in the lake
fishing soothes him
good for the soul
meditative, restorative
46 years together

trees cover the mountains
the water in the lake
rippling like random rows
crystalline threads
all travelling one way

ground squirrels beg for food
countenances perfect
in praying position
eyes bright, beseeching

a baby cries
nearby at a picnic table
clouds begin to mask the sun
this lovely June day
we both feel renewed

I remember many picnics
daughters and dog
trees and waves
hold all these memories
safely in leaves and splashes

love for Don and daughters
on the gentle breeze
laps at my face
through the open window
light beginning to fade
the afternoon progresses
like me

I hold on to that light
fiercely
daughters grown
building lives with amazing men

the dog's ashes rest
among our photos
the hot dogs he buried here
at Manning long gone
no doubt pounced upon
by ground squirrels
scrabbling, digging
amazed at their unbelievable luck

these places of love
memory
longing

Slope of a Curve

(for Lana)

love is not
Purdy's chocolate

Valentine's Day cards
bouquets of hothouse flowers

fuchsia lingerie from Victoria's Secret
dinner out with candlelight and a bottle of Prosecco

    but enough with all love is not, like
    other poets, I too will count the ways of love

love is the eight thousand walks, hikes, bike rides
we have traced, learning how to breathe light

love is the forty-eight thousand meals we have savoured,
most prepared by you with Julia Child's culinary eagerness

love is the sixteen thousand nights we have slept
often knotted in one another's arms and legs

love is parenting children who still mesmerize us with
their wild imaginations, their fondness for adventures

love is learning to be Nana and Papa, enthralled
by the ineffable energy of vivacious granddaughters

love is seeing you, remembering the first time, easily
millions of times, still astonished by you

love is never running out of stories, never taking
for granted the stories that have run out

love is the calculus of continuous change, how the slope
of a curve is never the same, but always familiar

love is the fruit of the spirit, a heavenly vintage
called into dazzling delight by tender, firm hands

Wedding Over

teacups unpacked
I pore through photos
not that I need prompts

I remember your hair pinned back
that maroon flower
your elegant dress
selected with your sisters and me
bearing witness

how you asked me
to walk you
down the cottage stairs
me limping, uneven stone
ceremony on grass carpet
Island foliage
not to give you away
physically you left long ago
you never were mine to own
mothers live on borrowed time
but oh, you are of my body
my love fierce
the walk your gift to me

I remember how you cried
exchanging rings with Mike
this brilliant funny man
your loving golden words so deep
gentle like you
your tears mine
my tears yours

the way you hugged me
after the ceremony
during the dinner
throughout the incredible night
you crying
when I read my poem to you
you'd heard it before
but wept anyway

in a sister's slideshow
you looking in a mirror
did you see all this then?
dressed up as a miniature bride
at 2
and painting at an easel
wearing your father's shirt
dragging on the floor

and later
lying on your cottage bed
laughing about the lost rental spoon
it was nowhere
we looked everywhere
until I said
I'd rather pay for the damn thing
wedding at an end
so much more to search out

Always on My Mind

like Willy Nelson
vocation is
always on my mind

Papa Poet Professor

three P's in a pod

invited to live in the world

living vocation
all the time

I am
a living vocation

I will never get it right
there is no *it* to get right

I want the ludic, the play
without illusion and delusion

teaching is not a sexy Siren
who seduced me
to dash against the rocks

teaching is a saxophone
with a poignant call
to find the way

amidst prepositional possibilities
for living in the world
amidst words

The Day I Set the Kitchen on Fire

I was making soup
I love a pot of homemade
in the fridge
I have a whole soup making
history:
beef, chicken, turkey
minestrone
pea

just one minute distracted
the tiler calling me
from the bathroom renovation
upstairs
I had daughters on my mind
my mother's unveiling
stupid, stupid, stupid
you don't leave a pot
unattended
had I reached my quota
attending to daughters?

the screech of alarm
the flames leaping
from pot to vent
vent to cupboards
the sick feeling
in my stomach
guilty, guilty, guilty

Don smothered the fire
with a lid
heroic
the tiler came running too
Mother's Day gift idea
a new pot

I'm not yet ready
for the Home
it's not like you
daughters say
oblivious to recent fights
the smoke filling the rooms
my heart
swirling in complicated patterns
forming black cobwebs
spiderless
little Miss Muffet
would not have liked these either

soot drifting
like my thoughts
landing in the oddest places
soup, daughters, mothers
a mishmash

Snow Geese

at the Steveston Hotel Café
Laura and I discuss poetry
loss   trauma   blessings

Laura asks, are those seagulls?
silver birds with dark wing tips
hover outside the expansive window

(perhaps ducks, I wonder how many
birds live near the Gulf of Georgia)
Laura notes, they're snow geese

just the day before I had walked
to Garry Point, everywhere snow geese
I didn't see, or at least didn't look

even though I grew up with
Dick's reminding Sally
        Look, look.
        Look up.
        Look up, up, up.

gap of poetic awareness
caught up in whirling busyness
saturated   inattentive   senseless

knowing how little I know,
will ever know, I will heed
Dick's wisdom and look, look

Critic in Flight

bones
falling out of the sky
dropped on Aeschylus'
bald pate
tragically killing him
the lamagaya bird
looking for a place to splinter dinner
thought the playwright's head
was a rock
vision not being its strong point
or perhaps
it was a point of criticism
delivered the only way the bird could
straight from the mouth
to the head

Love Is

(Lana, January 7, 2019)

Love is joking around,
even finding my way
in words when the words
are popping up like gophers

Love is walking a tightrope
of remembering and dreaming,
always tense with balance,
singing with rhythm

Love is the blank space
that just called out to me
to continue writing
whatever called out

Love is letting go with
a stream of green ink flowing
from my fountain pen like I can
row my boat to the earth's centre

Love is calling out, even quietly,
while I wait for an answer
that might never come, or
might come, full of surprises

Love is one more stanza, always,
a stanza like a dais, a platform
for shaping views so we can
see what needs to be seen

Love is knowing the mystery
at the heart of every tunnel,
with mazes here and there,
always hopeful for …

Here in This Meadow

(for Rebecca)

you play your flute
piccolo
the notes whirl high as we sing
Matt plays bass
a deep steady pulse
proud
I feel so blessed
you found each other

the second sopranos ask me
how many instruments
does Rebecca play?
I list bassoon, contra bassoon
saxophone and more

but you are even more than musician
dog lover
gardener
environmentalist
scientist
jewelry maker
potter
crocheter

and now
loving partner to a wonderful man

here in this meadow
among us
you chant your vows
promise
the love and hope of the future
wildflowers singing in your garden
your heart

Surprising Grace

1

my day was filled with Spirit's surprises:
  a blessing of growing old is learning
  to enjoy each moment for what it is

2

I am generally suspicious of rationality
especially when rationality is presented
as syllogism (with no attention to silliness)
or cognition (with no recognition of cogitation)
or mastery (with no acknowledgement of mystery)

3

I have learned to speak about spirituality in the academy
from the example of Muslim students who speak openly
about prayer and God and divine love infusing human love

4

Madeleine said, *In Newfoundland a minute is only 30 seconds.*
I'm not sure what she meant, but I like the notion that time
is always different from what you expect. Time challenges
simple chronology. Like Spirit dwells in imagination to remind
us everything we know and do and are and are becoming is still
only partial, far more expansively mysterious than any story
we compose to explain ourselves to ourselves and others.

5

we often understand grace as something
we have, something we have inside us
like a seam of coal or a bank deposit
or a humor (as opposed to a tumor)

perhaps grace is not in us at all,
what if grace is the spirit
that holds all the creation
with rhythm and resonance

perhaps our calling is to bask in grace,
lean into grace, invite grace to permeate us,
hopefully trust that grace will hold us in the midst of everything that rattles
rankles wrestles us

6

Christians are so eager to deify Jesus
when we need to pay attention to reifying him
transmuting the abstract into the concrete

7

Saturday morning is a poetic space
for remembering the week
that has been, imagining
the week that might be

8

Christianity can be so unimaginatively fundamentalist
and theologically warped it is hard to wonder how

Christianity doesn't implode on its cultural expressions,
Christian fictions and misinterpreted myths

9

because Nana loves potato chips
she always gives them up for Lent

on Shrove Tuesday, Nana and I served pancakes
to Madeleine and Mirabelle while their parents went to the gym

in Newfoundland, Shrove Tuesday is Pancake Day,
and we have always enjoyed eating pancakes with money tucked inside

in the course of explaining Shrove Tuesday and Ash Wednesday and Lent
to Madeleine and Mirabelle, Nana explained her decision to give up potato chips

the next day, Madeleine's Mama reported that Madeleine had announced
she was giving up salsa and when her mother reminded her she doesn't eat salsa

Madeleine pointed out that sometimes she is served salsa
at the after-school Y program she attends on Monday and Friday

10

like poetry grammar is
a magical evocation of hopeful possibilities

how is grammar connected to
glamour magic alchemy spells spelling?

can any of us live without
grammar and the spell of poetry?

11

no day is complete without
reading and writing poetry!

12

did I really lose faith?   not likely
I live with faith   I hold steadfast to faith
I will not lose faith   faith grows   I hope
I want to shout at God   I imagine many people do
at least those who think he can hear   can even care
most people don't care   I care   I especially care
my brother is dead   all I have left are memories
stealing apples   throwing them at one another

13

a gull guards
my neighbour's backyard
croaks a warning
like a lighthouse beacon
steady vigilance even
in the absence of danger

Here Among the Trees

(for Sara)

who knew back then?
when Erin and Sam
graduated high school
wishing they were sisters
our families celebrated together
Sara there
David there

who knew?
when our families socialized
at Deb and Len's
Sara there
David there

who knew?
years later they would text
reconnect
fall in love

Sara, our daughter
so beautiful, creative
so many stories in her to tell
loving David

David
so steadfast, droll
we call him the dog whisperer
loving Sara

here among the trees
atop Grouse Mountain
we celebrate them
rejoice in a cord of connection
between past and present
all of us
anticipating the future

Sara loving David
David loving Sara

Santa Claus

(for Mirabelle)

when I was a child, long ago, I sneaked
into my parents' bedroom and found
a store of Christmas toys on top

of a shelf in a closet, dark and hidden,
tucked behind extra bed clothes
and towels from Duz detergent

faced with a crisis of faith, I knew
my parents were either Santa's elves
or, worse, there was no Santa at all

when Mirabelle was ten months old
she first met Santa at the Richmond Mall,
luxuriant, laughing beard, a Coca-Cola ad

but Mirabelle refused to sit in Santa's lap
and the next Christmas sat in her mother's lap
beside Santa but wouldn't smile for the camera

by the third Christmas Mirabelle still
refused Santa's invitations with a stern
unwillingness to play the game, but while

I held her in the long line, Santa dropped
over, here and there, to say hi, and when
he invited her again, Mirabelle finally

cuddled him with smiles, and Santa sidled
over and gave me a high five as we remembered
past Christmases, how belief is rooted in experience

Santa Claus was omniscient, loving, patient,
and with Mirabelle I believed in magic
steeped in myth and infectious possibility

Grandmother Tales

I hold June
Erin plays with Frances
who smiles and giggles
June cries a bit
making strange
a week since they've seen me

soon she settles
remembering
responds to my voice
my songs:
You are my sunshine
Rig a jig jig
and Ten in the bed

we switch babies
Frances coos and smiles
till Erin sleep-deprived
is off to nap
the babies now on their play mat
watching, listening
my every movement
every song

I give them rubber duckies
bought for bath time
they investigate
straight to their mouths
and I sing:
Rubber duckie
you're the one

you make bath time
so much fun

they look at me
as they play
happy to have singing Bubbee
gazing down at them
love and lyrics in the air

but woeful cries of hunger
eventually beckon
I prepare their bottles
the babies alert
the sound
of baby "cappuccino machine"
mixing
familiar
soothing

then two bottles
two hands (mine)
two twins
two feedings
propped up by their rattles
(I dub them Mrs. Rattleford)

it's a sporadic feed
June bounces
on the twinsie pillow
blowing milk bubbles
a double bubble baby bubble blower
Frances squirms
holds my finger
drinks, stops, splutters

temporarily I give up
take them to one of the cribs
side by side
they smile up at me
smiles that could melt misery
as I change them
happy to be together

we finish the feeding
me hunched over the crib rails
then one by one
I hold them
sing the lullabies that soothe

June falls asleep in my arms
heavy, lax with slumber
I lower her to her crib
hold Frances and sing
she sings along
ah, ah, ah, ah...
through three lullabies
ah, ah, ah...
with no interruptions
she is singing with me
celebrating granddaughters
grandmothers
until she too
lowered to her crib
startled cries out once
sighs
closes her eyes
asleep

The Spider

(for Mirabelle)

while searching for the etymology of *fantastic* I stumbled down the rabbit hole of the rhizomean internet, seduced by stories about Brad Pitt and Kim Kardashian, and stopped abruptly on a feature from *The Detroit News* about the 2017 Fiat 124 Spider, and remembered the car Saul drove in Stephenville when I was a teacher, in my twenties, kind of poor, but still making ends meet, dreaming about the future, learning how to be a father, and remembered how much I liked Saul's Spider—black, sleek, glistening, compact, fast—the kind of car smart, sophisticated people might drive, the kind of people you can now follow vicariously (even voraciously) on the internet for hours and hours, and I remembered how glad I was to leave Stephenville after six years of frenzied fundamentalism, and how much I would have enjoyed driving away in a Spider while I drove away in a Chevy Impala, loaded with family and stuff, on our way to new adventures (and what a lot of adventures there have been) and now, decades later Mazda bought Fiat or Fiat bought Mazda (or at least they are sharing body parts in a game of reckless or shrewd economic cohabitation), and the Spider has been re-invented and re-presented more than three decades after the last Spider was produced in 1985, the same year I left Stephenville, and I realize I haven't thought much about the Spider or about Stephenville since, but all these decades later, a new Spider has been manufactured, and I am suddenly the man who still wants one because the Spider (with its turbocharged, intercooled SOHC 16-valve inline-4 with 160 horsepower and 184 pound-feet of torque—all impressive, especially if you know what any of those specs actually mean) continues to spin a web in my imagination, a web connecting the past to the present like they are still staring one another in the crystal eye, but the new Spider is not the old Spider (the new Spider is really a Mazda Miata with the body of an Aurelio Lampredi-inspired Fiat—a lot like the elderly Jane Fonda still looks like Hanoi Jane or Barbarella) since the new Spider with its Italian Fiat curves is made in a Mazda plant in Hiroshima with a suspension designed by American engineers—the offspring of cosmopolitanism, corporatism, consumerism, and cultural compulsion—and while walking with my granddaughter Mirabelle (well, I was walking, and she was riding her skateboard—cool in the way a six-year old is cool), she saw an old two-seat roadster with the top down, and I'm suddenly dreaming about Lana and me driving fast up the Sea to Sky Highway on our way to Whistler as dusk settles on the Coast Mountains, the engine roaring romantically (dreaming doesn't get better than the dream I am dreaming) when Mirabelle looked long at the tiny, tight interior, at the two seats, and asked, Papa, where do the children sit?, and I knew then and there I will never drive a Spider, especially as I veer around a sharp curve on my way to the Richmond Auto Mall for a Dodge Caravan.

Thirteen Teacups

packed for the wedding
by special request
I choose their favourites
green with gold filigree
gold flecked with maroon
scalloped yellow
with flowers inside
and for me
gold & white
embellished
with the word Mother

each one different
so each person
knows theirs for the night

there is history here
bonds of grandmothers,
mothers, daughters

in the china cabinet
they are decorously stacked
my daughters admiring
looked through the glass brightly
as I once peered
what seems like
not so long ago

how is it
that tea tastes so much better
the wedding table so much
more adorned
this china art
this ancient ritual
these 13 connected collectibles
brimming
brushed by bliss

Hair

almost all my adult life I have had
long hair, a long time I have been my hair

I have had long hair for so long, I don't
know who I am without long hair

now diagnosed with cancer, I am assured
my hair will fall out with chemotherapy

I am quite startled by how quickly old age
crept up and whacked me in the head

a woman shampooed my hair once, massaged
my scalp so perfectly I fell in love with her

my four granddaughters all have long
flowing hair, they all like my hair, too

Samson, Absalom, Willie Nelson,
Tony Little, Karl Lagerfeld, Tarzan

Howie Mandell on the cover of *Zoomer*
happily looks good with a bald head

last summer a boy asked, are you a boy
or a girl? I said, I haven't decided yet

the Apostle Paul thinks long hair
on a man is a disgrace to him

Ujjal Dev Singh Dosanjh, Steven Tyler,
Wang Deshun, Randy Savage

occasionally in places like restaurants women
my age will caress my hair, I like your hair

in a world where I feel invisible most
of the time, I am always glad to be seen

in life one thing leads to another, so eventually
we see our lives plotted like lines on a graph

what will the future hold? always
hopeful there is some future

Pumpkins

the ghosts
of all those Hallowe'ens past
and now we are gathered
years later
carving
sharing recipes
one daughter decorating
like the house and yard
are her personal set design
the others content
to eat pumpkin soup
taste orange

the dog gone
 years ago
another casualty to memory
we laugh remembering
how he sensed the ritual
upped the chaos

you can regret
the passage of time
it won't change anything
I like the morphing
of traditions
adults once children
coming together
the seeds of all those pumpkins
planted *je ne sais quoi*

as I inhale the acrid scent of candles
burning pumpkin flesh
the little girl that was me
in a gypsy costume
rings and rings a Calgary doorbell
setting all this in motion

Sweet Digz Farm

on a sunny Saturday morning in November
after a long walk on the dike I stood
in line with Lana a long time in order to buy
fresh produce from Sweet Digz Farm

Kareno & Kimi operate a small-scale
organic farm in Steveston where the flats
of the Fraser River delta are fertile
for growing veggies, seed, and herbs

one time I would have balked at waiting
in line so long to buy a few brussels sprouts
but not anymore, now I wait patiently
or at least mostly patiently, glad to be alive

why is the woman banging into me with her bag?
why is she reaching around me to feel the kale
that she can feel all she wants as soon as
I move forward in the line? why did she just knock

over several bottles of coriander and break
a few without apology? why is this woman
such a nuisance? why does my patience not
extend to her? all good questions on this odd

Saturday morning when all I can really think
about is the appointment with Dr. Shen
on Monday morning when she will explain
the new plans for further chemotherapy

since the old plans did not work as well
as we had hoped and even believed
how does one's life become wrapped up
in illness so there is no stillness?

how does one's life take a sharp detour
around a corner you didn't even see?
how does one's life change overnight
so you hardly recognize the man in the mirror?

I want to enjoy the moments of standing
in line on a Saturday morning without
any concern about what else I ought to be doing,
where else I should be, how else I might be

I just want to enjoy looking at people, odd in countless
ways, in splendid idiosyncrasies, bald heads,
efforts at romance, spun illusions, eager for
fresh produce, dreams of urbanity amidst the rural

Mother May I

thank you for years of love
you were not perfect
I didn't expect that
once I threw my children's easel
across the room

I am eating hot buttered popcorn,
mother
your favourite
and by the way
it was not me
who ate that tuna sandwich
and what does that matter
anyway?

remember how
you put the coffee table decoration I gave you
on the kitchen table
after our fight

when we walked together
you noticed I was limping
I hadn't said a word

I am using your hand towel, mother
threadbare but I hold it
to my face
and your face appears
I am brushing my hair
with your yellow brush
feel your roots

I'm wearing your ring
it fits perfectly
I feel the weight of your hand

sometimes I walk
through my living room
past your china cabinet
your coffee tables
feel you there
you let my children
play on those tables
then complained
their toys could scratch the finish
I love those scratches
heirloom memories
I know that back and forth too

we are planning your unveiling,
mother
in the hot summer Calgary sun
I will read a poem, a prayer
we will uncover the headstone
place stones on your grave
and dad's
remember
your blue and white coffin
an Israeli flag of grief
lowered into the ground

mother may I
thank you for the years of love

Heron

the world is falling apart
and my response is to write
another poem about
the heron I saw this morning
while walking the dike beside
the Fraser River when perhaps
I should write about salmon
daily disappearing, or hiding,
or Japanese Canadians
who once fished here but
learned with war they were
more Japanese than Canadian
even if they were born in
Steveston, British Columbia,
and know as much about Japan
as the rest of us who grew up
on Hollywood war films,
or I should write about urban
sprawl or agrarian disaster
or untreated sewage or the earth
quake that will one day wash
all Lulu Island into the Gulf
of Georgia like a memory
too proud of itself, but no
I write again about the heron
standing still in the river
as if I know anything at all
about herons, since taught
forever by Walt Disney
to anthropomorphize wildness,
I imagine countless stories

for the heron, but know
only the heron's otherness
and utter disregard for me
watching it like a creature
with nothing better to do
while the world falls apart
and I write another poem
about the heron I saw
standing alone in the grass
on the edge of the river
waiting for a fish or a bug
minding its own business

CNN Redux

KIDNAP VICTIMS ESCAPE!
WOMAN WHO KILLED HER BOYFRIEND IN A JEALOUS RAGE
SPEAKS TO THE JURY!
TORNADO WHIPS THROUGH OKLAHOMA!

we view photos of the captives
hear from
neighbours mothers
shocked
imagine those chains

we listen to a murderer
plead for death
then life
she thinks a recycling program
will convince a jury
she deserves not to die
it's difficult to gauge the sincerity

we witness emotional reunions
with children at demolished schools
death tolls mark children who perished
along with school walls
tears for teachers

every last detail
unearthed from stories
a ticker tape of tidbits
moves across the screen
an escalator to a shop of horrors

reporters commiserate
compassion underscores the sensational
from their screen to your head
loyalty shifts
each breaking story
ascends the litany ladder:
loss, licentiousness, love
this triumvirate of L's
reminds us
humans fail
nature is a fickle parent
tragedy kindles hope

STILL WRITING

is life at the end of the alphabet different
from life at the beginning of the alphabet?
Carl Leggo

Diagnosis

seven months ago I was diagnosed with non-Hodgkin's lymphoma,
and five months ago I was diagnosed with a brain tumour

it is hard to live with the prospect of a short life,
at least a life shorter than I generally anticipated

on this Friday morning at the end of November
I recall the brain biopsy, at least a little,

and I will never forget the six cycles of chemotherapy
in the BC Cancer Agency where I stayed for five days

each cycle, and received many injections and transfusions
and tender care from committed medical professionals

and the hopes for stem cell therapy buoyed me up for a time
till I was told the therapy would be postponed

because the non-Hodgkin's lymphoma was still prevalent
and virulent and had to be attended to first

and now I am undergoing four cycles of chemotherapy
called CHOP-R that will hopefully diminish the lymphoma

but the challenge is keeping up my spirits, especially
in spite of all the hope and prayer and love that sustains me

even while I ache with discomfort in my head and weariness
in my body, and my spirit feels squashed, at least a little,

I don't really know how I feel any more—perhaps just confused
like I wish I knew how the story would end, even when it will end,

that is how I feel, like I am now lost, out of control, no longer
writing my story, as if I ever actually wrote my story,

perhaps I feel like the story is emerging in the hands of others,
and I don't know if I can trust those hands, too much disappointment,

if somebody told me I had ten more years to live I could be
content, and I would make plans for living another decade

even if somebody told me I had ten more months to live I could
at least clean out my office and say good-bye and hug my family
but I really have no idea if I will live a few months, a few years,
a few decades, instead I now think I am not so much living as dying

and that is not satisfying—I do not think I was born to die,
I was born to live and perhaps encourage others to live

diagnosis is the discovery of an illness, based on symptoms,
recognizing, discerning, distinguishing, knowing the parts

when I look in the mirror, who do I see?
not the person I remember, who I think I am, might be

instead I see an old man who has lived a long time,
made plenty of mistakes, some very big mistakes,

a person who carries his guilt like a sack of rocks around his neck,
a man who can still smile wryly like he knows life has been good

in spite of every thing that has unfolded in the fabric of his daily life
like lint and old tissues and shapes and wrinkles that remind

me I am old and used, how I should now relax in my quiet living room
and read the last few books I most want to read and write another poem or two

and look forward to saying good-bye to family and colleagues and friends
who have inspirited my life with joy and hope and lovely rhythms

am I brave enough to embrace the possibility of death, or am I
just defeated? have I ever really loved life enough to deserve it?

have I been waiting since birth for the climactic signature, The End,
or have I been waiting for the story to unfold so I know who I am?

perhaps that is the hardest part of dying—not so much losing all the joys
of daily life, of family and routines and rituals and celebrations

but realizing all your hopes have now drawn to a kind of close
and hence why heaven looms so big and bright as the last hope

what would unfold in this poem if I really started
writing about my frustration, sadness, sense of loss?

I am an old man, apparently worn out, even though
there is no reason why I should expect to live a long life

especially when so many people do not live long lives
like my brother who died at sixty-two

so many people dying all the time, beginning to think
our stories are about to take off, surprised they are over,

I was looking at another five years of work at UBC,
a few more books of poetry, finishing up with graduate students,

sorting out my books and office, making a little extra money
and taking the whole family to Disneyland

but really those potential five years are not very important!
I have lived a (mostly) happy life, and I am grateful for all,

especially happy to have enjoyed my life with Lana
and Anna and Aaron and Nick and Penny

and Madeleine and Mirabelle and Gwenoviere and Alexandria,
I am content, I will embrace whatever emerges as my life story

Legacy

my granddaughters sleep
on their twinsie pillow
hands askew
open to the world

a sigh
a flutter of eyelids
a turn of a head

each breath
fills me with such joy
each day with them a gift

the pains that come with aging
subside as I hold, rock
breathe in, feed babies

I think of you, Carl
I sent you photos, poems
beautiful you replied
once you held babies too
your children
grandchildren
how you have loved them
caressed them with poems
heartfelt
your legacy
you are in them

always
I think of you, Carl
ache for the unwritten poems

Waiting

in the season of Lent each day is
jam-packed and I wait restlessly

while astronomers recently found
evidence for a theoretical perspective

Einstein proposed a century ago
regarding gravitational waves

that emerged after two black holes
touched 1.3 billion years ago

what is a moment, a day, a week,
a century, even 1.3 billion years?

what are forty 40 days
in the mystery of creation?

I live like an impatient patient
in the emergency ward of a hospital

with little hospitality when I want
to learn to wait and lean into

the moment, both now and new,
ancient and iterative, always

Still Writing

I can imagine you
writing a poem about dying
how it snowed that day
how you let go
even though you wrote
in a paper:
you wanted
to take your whole family
to Disneyland
wanted to write letters
to everyone
wanted to be there
for your grandchildren
not yet finished mourning
your brother

even though
you and I
were collecting our poems
planning a sequel

the last time I saw you
we read poems from our book:
relationships
daughters granddaughters
your son
our mothers
Virginia Woolf
joy loss disruption hope
all the good stuff
you would say

your poem would be moving
full of the heart we have come
to know
in your words
and raw with emotion
life writing
death writing
oh so profound

I will imagine you
surrounded by the alphabet
whirling
in clouds
having unravelled the knot of fear
you wrote about
with the fingers of poetry

still writing poems

Nine Meditations in the Dentist's Chair

1
in the liminal space of February
I take stock like a shopkeeper:
  go to the dentist
  buy tires for the CRV
  remember colleagues
  who might need prayer

2
beginning the day
with a root canal
    reminds me
    how much
    I love life

3
there are
    many kinds of love
and I have been blessed
    to know some,
    likely far more
        than many
but long love
    lasting love
love shaped on a last
    is the love
I thank God for
    daily

4
we join God
            in prayer
not because we need
to remind God
or persuade God
or cajole God
like an inattentive parent
checking Facebook
but because God
invites us to enter
the divine energy
of endless creation

5
sitting in Dr. Carter's chair
I pray for friends:
            Harry is dying in Maple Ridge
Regina is living with cancer
            William is dying in North Van
            Doris is living with cancer

6
Carrie claims nothing means
            anything anymore
but doesn't everything mean
            something, perhaps
we have forgotten how to be

7
prayer is a way of breathing
oxygen   spirit   pneuma

prayer is a way of leaning into
the world, refusing to surrender

8
at a conference in San Francisco
with thousands of other educators
    one colleague said, I am
    suspicious of anyone
    who talks about hope

9
on this gray wet day in Lent
while the world rotates
with slow heavy rhythms,
I offer a brief prayer
as I remember you fondly,
often, a hallowed haunting

Echo Chamber

I'm listening in the car
Leonard Cohen's Hallelujah
reverberates
my favourite
and I cry
remembering this is the song
you chose for your funeral
four months ago

you are in good company
Patrick Lane, Joe Rosenblatt
died the same day, week
this death of poets
this poetic stoppage

I have your last poems
ones you wrote
as you faced death
as you walked through that valley
Hallelujah, hallelujah

I will read them, commit them
to this book
weave them in and out
among my words
this echo chamber
thrumming with lives lived
lives lost
echo location
Hallelujah, hallelujah

Advice for Living the Quotidian

for sixty-five years I wish I had known
how short life is, too short, impossibly brief

how to live each moment as momentous,
alive in each moment with hope for possibility

light and shadow dance a tango, everything
in flow, everything likely or unlikely

this poem reminds me to listen carefully,
to remember with the body's story

everything is heightened, everything is dull,
cancer refracts light in unknown ways

a poet begins with sitting, perhaps
on a bench or a rock, under a tree

our first poem is the heart's beat, breathing
is the ancient language we must always hear

each day requires sensual attending
and taken-for-granted assumptions

I now seek to maintain a balance
between intensity and relaxation

if you want people to smile, smile at them
if you want a hug, offer a hug

above all, be sure to untangle the knot
of fear that threatens to strangle you

a poem is a response to silence,
the quiet resonance that lingers

poets are not scared to know the sacred, each
day brings blessings like disguised challenges

learn to lean on uncertainty,
know the journey is a mystery

be open to surprises, the stuff
of creation, new beginnings

hold the whole of life,
holes and all, heart-wide

always move with rhythm
like a carpenter's sure swing

if you want to know how to live
then live with love's tenderness

waiting with autumn patience for
the fullness after emptiness

this is all the wisdom I have to offer,
a broken body knows a lifetime

the mortal dances with the immortal,
heaven and earth in a kingdom of joy

Afterword

Years ago at UBC poet & professor Carl Leggo encouraged me to embark upon what became for me a transformative writing journey.

I wrote the following poetry books published by Inanna Publications, with the encouragement of and support of the late Luciana Ricciutelli , Editor in Chief of Inanna, who I miss:

True Confessions (awarded a Canadian Jewish Book Award)
Martha in the Mirror
Backhand Through the Mother

Then Carl & I together wrote *Hearing Echoes* and now, *Echo Chamber*, (Innana Publications) books that moved between his poems & mine.

Sadly Carl passed away. He is missed.

Acknowledgements

In addition to my daughters Sara, Rebecca, & Erin, I thank my partner Don for all his love and support and tolerance over the years.

Additional thank you's to my machatunim,

Elaine & John, Deb & Len

And my sisters Estelle & Patty
And sons-in law Mike, David, & Matt

And for granddaughter Ellee, a poem:
Ellee Ellee Ellee
Milkie in your belly
You're so sweet
What a treat
Ellee Ellee Ellee
Can't have deli

COVID grand baby
You arrive during a pandemic
Reminding all of us
How precious you are
A miracle
A blessing
That life goes on
Even if we close our circles
Chuck wagons against virus

You are oblivious
To the risks
Sleep

(Mostly in our arms)
Drink your mama's milk
Some top up
So mama can sleep
Spit up
Especially fun
On a fresh sheet
Fart like an adult
We laugh at the sound and smell
From such a tiny being
Hold your poos
Then explode
All over everything

And now you look
Into my eyes
Smile when I sing
Hush you bye
Don't you cry
Baby beluga
The bottle nipple
In your mouth
You "talk" to me
I imagine
You are thanking me
For the milk

Till mama wakes up
Telling me stories
Your stroller walk
The drive in the car seat
Dada's night shift with you
The world so new to you
Born during social distancing
Marathon hand washing

Your twin cousins
Peek at you in the car
Drive by Ellee
Your auntie calls it
Your aunties (once my babies)
In the yard
Six feet away

Still we can feel the connection
The bonds of love
Celebrate you
Wish we could all hug
Hope for the future

Anna & Alistair, your poems to come.

Thank you to Lana Verge (Carl Leggo's spouse) & their children Anna & Aaron for their help with the details of publication.

Thank you to colleagues & friends Erika Hasebe-Ludt, Lynn Fels, Bonnie Nish, Kedrick James, & George Belliveau for their responses to Echo Chambers.

And in memory of Luciana Ricciutelli who is missed.

Thank you Debra Bell & Inanna Publications for the opportunity to share Carl's & my poetry.

About the Authors

Renee Norman , PhD, is a prize-winning poet, writer and retired educator. Her poetry book, True Confessions (Inanna Publications) was awarded the Helen & Stan Vine Canadian Jewish book award for poetry. She is also the author of the poetry books: *Backhand Through the Mother, Martha in the Mirror*, & *Hearing Echoes*, also Inanna Publications. Renee's doctoral dissertation *House of Mirrors* was published as a book by Peter Lang Publishing. Her dissertation received the Canadian Association for Curriculum Studies Distinguished Dissertation Award. Her poetry, stories and articles have been published widely in literary and academic journals, anthologies, and newspapers. She has written for the Vancouver Sun and taught at both UBC and Simon Fraser University as a sessional lecturer. Renee lives in Coquitlam, BC. with her partner.

Carl Leggo lived, taught, and wrote in the Vancouver area until his death in 2019. Drawing from his memories of an adventurous childhood in Newfoundland, he wove humorous, heartfelt tales into poetic ruminations that formed the first of his many published books. After studying in various cities across Canada and earning his PhD, Carl moved to Vancouver in 1990 and began a decades-long career in the Faculty of Education at UBC, where he left a lasting impression on students and colleagues alike. When he passed away, a memorial held at UBC drew a crowd of people whose lives he had so meaningfully touched.More than anything, Carl was a husband, father, and grandfather whose family still misses and thinks of him every day. His profound presence and creative spirit live on in his writing.